DK READERS

Level 1

Level 2

A Note to Parents

DK READERS is a compelling program for beginning readers, designed in conjunction with leading literacy experts, including Dr. Linda Gambrell, Distinguished Professor of Education at Clemson University. Dr. Gambrell has served as President of the National Reading Conference, the College Reading Association, and the International Reading Association.

Beautiful illustrations and superb full-color photographs combine with engaging, easy-to-read stories to offer a fresh approach to each subject in the series. Each DK READER is guaranteed to capture a child's interest while developing his or her reading skills, general knowledge, and love of reading.

The five levels of DK READERS are aimed at different reading abilities, enabling you to choose the books that are exactly right for your child:

Pre-level 1: Learning to read
Level 1: Beginning to read
Level 2: Beginning to read alone
Level 3: Reading alone
Level 4: Proficient readers

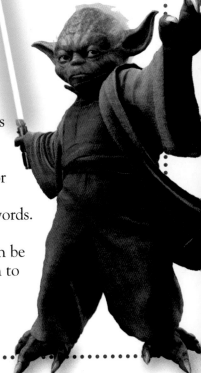

The "normal" age at which a child begins to read can be anywhere from three to eight years old. Adult participation through the lower levels is very helpful for providing encouragement, discussing storylines, and sounding out unfamiliar words.

No matter which level you select, you can be sure that you are helping your child learn to read, then read to learn!

LONDON, NEW YORK, MUNICH,
MELBOURNE, and DELHI

Senior Editor Laura Gilbert
Senior Designer Lisa Sodeau
Managing Art Editor Ron Stobbart
Publishing Manager Catherine Saunders
Art Director Lisa Lanzarini
Publisher Simon Beecroft
Publishing Director Alex Allan
Pre-production Producer Andy Hilliard
Producer Kara Wallace

Lucasfilm
Executive Editor J.W. Rinzler
Keeper of the Holocron Leland Chee
Art Director Troy Alders
Director of Publishing Carol Roeder

Reading Consultant
Linda B. Gambrell, Ph.D.

First published in the United States in 2012
by DK Publishing
345 Hudson Street
New York, New York 10014
13 14 15 10 9 8 7 6 5 4 3 2

004-182940-Nov/2012

DK books are available at special discounts when purchased in bulk
for sales promotions, premiums, fund-raising, or educational use.
For details, contact: DK Publishing Special Markets, 345 Hudson
Street, New York, New York 10014
SpecialSales@dk.com

A catalog record for this book is availablefrom the Library of
Congress.

ISBN: 978-07566-9808-9 (Paperback)
ISBN: 978-07566-9809-6 (Hardcover)
Color reproduction by Alta Image
Printed and bound in China by L-Rex Printing Co., Ltd.

Discover more at
www.dk.com

www.starwars.com

Contents

DK READERS

BEGINNING
1
TO READ

STAR WARS

WHO SAVED THE GALAXY?

Written by Catherine Saunders

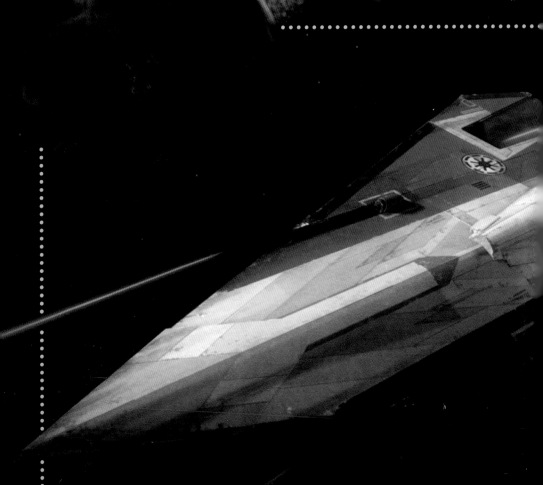

Dangerous times

The galaxy has faced
many troubles.

Most people want peace.

But some people want
to start wars.

Who can keep the galaxy safe?
It is a dangerous job. . . .

The Jedi

The Jedi believe in peace
and justice.

The Jedi Council

However, sometimes even
the Jedi must fight to keep
the galaxy safe.

During the Battle of Geonosis,
many brave Jedi fought
to defeat the Separatists
and their droid army.

Obi-Wan
Kenobi

Obi-Wan Kenobi

Jedi Knight Obi-Wan Kenobi
was known as "the Negotiator."

He was also a brave fighter.

He defeated a Sith called
Darth Maul in a duel.

Obi-Wan fought against
the Dark Sith Lord called
Darth Vader in a battle.

Obi-Wan sacrificed his own
life so that the galaxy
could be saved.

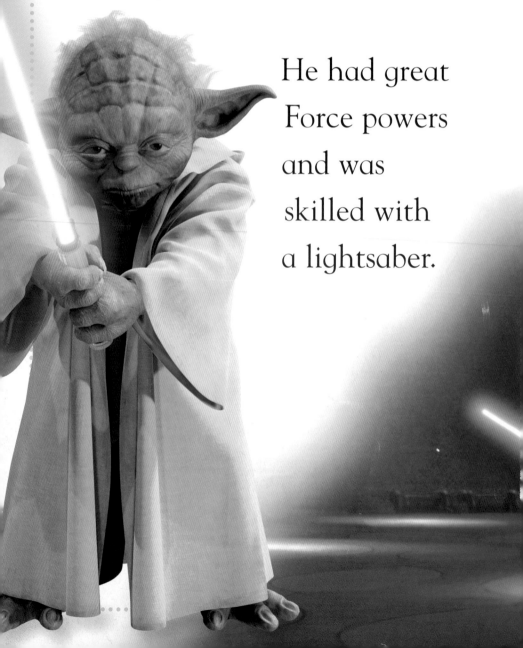

Master Yoda

This brave Jedi saved the galaxy many times.

He had great
Force powers
and was
skilled with
a lightsaber.

He dueled the Sith Lords
Dooku and Palpatine.

Yoda also trained many Jedi,
including Luke Skywalker.

Dooku ——————

The Clone Army

During the Clone Wars,
the Clone Army fought side by
side with the Jedi.

Each trooper was
brave, obedient,
and identical.

protective
armor

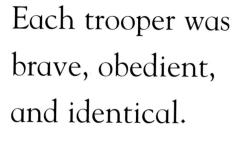

However,
the troopers had
a secret master.

At his command
they changed from
saving the galaxy to
helping to destroy it.

The rebels

The Rebel Alliance are
a very brave group of people.

They risked their lives to free
the galaxy from the evil
Emperor Palpatine.

The rebels destroyed both
the Emperor's superweapons
called the Death Stars.

They showed the people of
the galaxy that they did not
need to live in fear any more.

R2-D2

Princess Leia

Leia is a princess
and a senator from the
planet Alderaan.

She is also a rebel leader.

Princess Leia risked her life
many times to save the galaxy.

She helped the rebels
to destroy both Death Stars.

Han Solo

Some people don't mean
to save the galaxy.

Han Solo was a smuggler,
not a hero.

He helped the Rebel Alliance
on one mission.

Soon after, he was helping them to defeat Emperor Palpatine.

Chewbacca

Han Solo

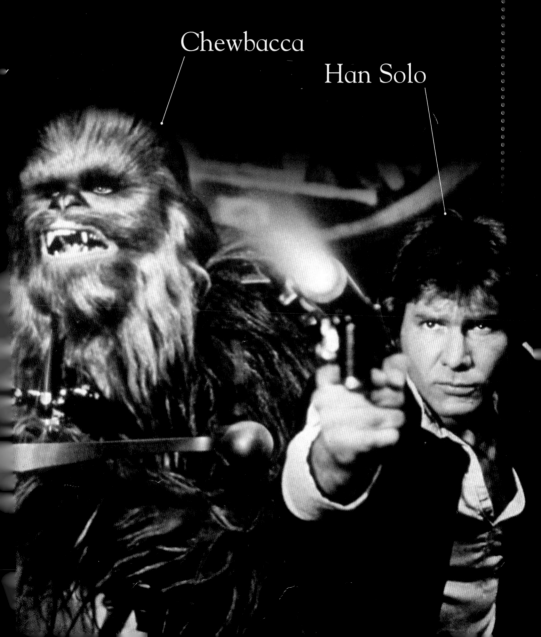

Anakin Skywalker

Anakin Skywalker was one of
the greatest Jedi ever known.

He first saved the galaxy
when he was
a young boy.

R2-D2

Later, Anakin became
a Jedi Knight and went
on many missions.

However, Anakin
was not able to
resist the power
of the dark side.

belt

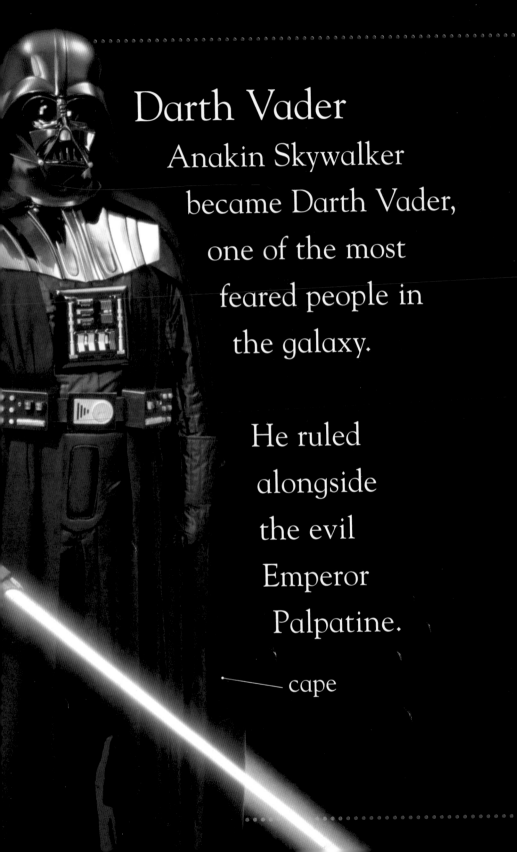

Darth Vader

Anakin Skywalker
became Darth Vader,
one of the most
feared people in
the galaxy.

He ruled
alongside
the evil
Emperor
Palpatine.

—— cape

When the Emperor tried to
attack Darth Vader's son, Luke,
Vader destroyed Palpatine.

Darth Vader saved Luke.

He also freed the galaxy from
the Emperor.

Luke Skywalker

Luke Skywalker is a Jedi.
He became part of
the Rebel Alliance.

He fired the shot that destroyed
the first Death Star.

Luke had the strength to resist
the power of the dark side.

His courage helped to unite
the galaxy. He even fought
Darth Vader.

The Ewoks

These small, furry creatures
don't look like they could save
the galaxy!

However, they helped
the rebels to defeat
Emperor Palpatine.

The Ewoks attacked Imperial
stormtroopers. This meant
the rebels could attack
the Death Star.

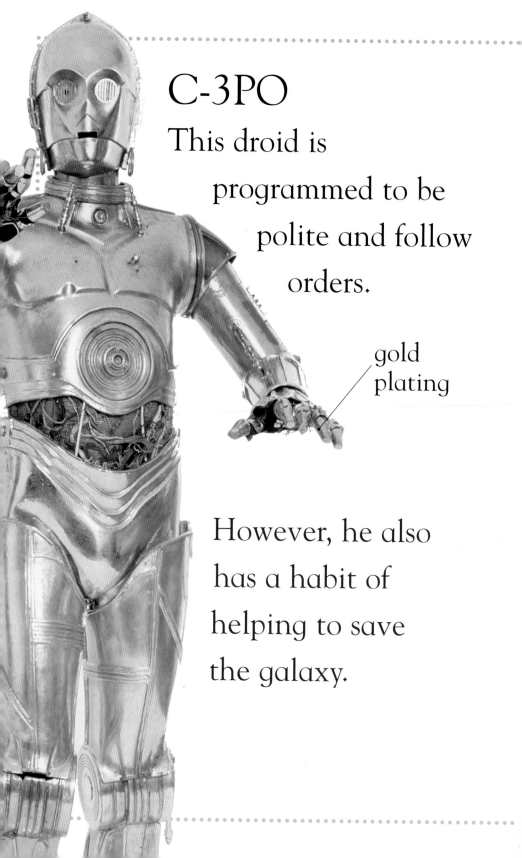

C-3PO

This droid is programmed to be polite and follow orders.

gold plating

However, he also has a habit of helping to save the galaxy.

It was C-3PO who convinced
the Ewoks to help the Jedi.

He happened to look just like
an Ewok god!

R2-D2

R2-D2 is a very brave and clever droid.

He can co-pilot spaceships, and fix them.

R2-D2 helped Anakin
Skywalker, Princess
Leia, and Luke
Skywalker to save
the galaxy.

Who do you
think truly saved
the galaxy?

Glossary

Dark side
The part of the Force associated with fear and hatred.

Droid army
A group of droids who fight. Droids are a type of robot.

Dueled
Fought, or battled.

Force powers
The energy created by all living things.

Jedi
People who can sense the energy created by all living things. This energy is called the Force.

Jedi Council
A group of Jedi and Jedi Masters who oversee all the other Jedi.

Lightsaber
A weapon that looks like a sword and has a blade made of pure energy.

Negotiator
Someone who discusses something in order to reach an agreement.

Obedient
Following orders. Willing to obey.

Sacrificed
Given up something for the sake of something else that's considered to be more worthy.

Separatists
A group of people who want to separate themselves from the Galactic Republic.

Sith
Enemies of the Jedi who use the dark side of the Force.

Smuggler
Someone who takes goods to a country or planet illegally.

Index

DK READERS

My name is

_____

I have read this book

Date

_____

E SAUND   RIN
Saunders, Catherine.
Star Wars, who saved the galaxy? /

RING
01/14